Natural Soaps with Essential Oils

by Ann Sullivan

Published in USA by:

Ann Sullivan
217 N. Seacrest Blvd #9
Boynton Beach
FL 33425

© Copyright 2017

ISBN-13: 978-1546526148
ISBN-10: 1546526145

Table of Contents

Introduction

If you've ever considered making the switch from store-bought soap to your own DIY soap only to second-guess the quality and effectiveness of homemade bodycare products, think again. Not only can you produce a high quality at-home natural product, but the process is quick and easy and can save you money in the long run. You'll also be able to customize your product per your body's needs and your own personal scent preferences, while avoiding all those harmful toxins found in consumer brands.

Believe it or not, your average store-bought soap is laden with synthetic chemicals that are damaging to your health. One of the toxins found in many commercial soaps? Sodium lauryl sulfate. This chemical has been shown not only to damage the skin, but has even been tied to cancer. By reacting with other ingredients, sodium lauryl sulfate is key to forming a nitrosamine called NDELA, which is a known carcinogen. When you use soap containing nitrosamine, your body absorbs the carcinogen at much higher levels than digesting it might. Though the FDA has cracked down on soap manufacturers in an attempt to control the levels of dioxin formation (another carcinogen compound) in those products with sodium lauryl sulfate, only by testing the product in a lab might one discover whether or not the soap contains abnormal levels of the carcinogen.

Sodium lauryl sulfate is not the only toxin in your soap. Another unfriendly ingredient in commercial soaps and in many bodycare products are parabens. Parabens are linked to breast cancer, appearing in a whopping 99% of breast cancer tissue. They've also been shown to contribute to Alzheimer's. So if you're hoping to skip those two, avoiding these toxic chemicals in your bodycare products will go a long way.

Why are these ingredients so destructive? Primarily because they're easily absorbed through the skin, which is of course where we apply most bodycare products. Once the toxic ingredients enter the skin, they're pulled into the bloodstream and circulated throughout the body, free to interfere in the functions of various organs, as well as with your body's natural chemistry.

So how can you avoid these toxins, while still producing an effective natural soap? Well, there are three general methods to produce handmade bar soap: melt-and-pour, hand-milled, or cold-pressed.

For the relatively new melt-and-pour method, you will create a "glycerin" or "casting" soap through the simple process of melting a pre-made block of base soap and pouring it into a mold, adding preferred scents, botanicals, or colors into the mix. The melt-and-pour method is the youngest, having been around only since the 19th century, and it creates an easily customizable transparent soap. The process can be completed in one hour.

The hand-milled method is a combination of the melt-and-pour and cold-pressed methods. In this process, you will be "re-batching" pre-made soap, by grating the all natural bars and melting them. In this way, you can customize your soap while avoiding working with harsh chemicals like lye. Arriving at a good consistency with this technique takes practice, and the process requires a few hours to produce the soap and four or five weeks to cure it.

Lastly, the cold-pressed method usually involves the previously-mentioned chemical, lye. By mixing a lye-water mixture with an oil combination, you will create a chemical reaction called saponification, which combines your ingredients into a gentle, cleansing soap. This bar creates glycerin as a by-product, which is a natural emollient. Of the three methods, the cold-pressed method will likely take the longest and require the most safety precautions. As with the hand-milled method, the soap will need to sit for at least a month to cure before use.

In this book, we've included recipes for liquid hand soap and dish soap as well. The melt-and-pour method is often utilized when producing these.

Before you get started, read all safety instructions in chapter 5. We'll also discuss the harmful toxins found in commercial soaps and those natural ingredients with which you can substitute commercial toxins. Doing so will not only help you limit the synthetic chemicals in your life, but can also serve to actively benefit your health.

Chapter 1:
Things You Don't Want to Put in Your Body: Potentially Dangerous Ingredients in Commercial Soaps

As mentioned in the introduction, commercial soaps contain more than their fair share of potentially dangerous ingredients, all of which can easily be avoided when producing your own homemade, natural product. Below, the harmful ingredients found most commonly in store-bought soaps are highlighted.

Sodium Lauryl Sulfate

As also described in the intro, sodium lauryl sulfate has been shown to damage skin cells and has been linked to cancer. And, yet, this toxic chemical is present in a large percentage of store-bought soaps. On top of these adverse effects, sodium lauryl sulfate has also been shown to interfere with eye development, particularly in children. The chemical impairs the formation of protein in the eye tissue of the young and may result in cataract formation. It is not necessary for the chemical to directly enter the eye to damage it; the systemic absorption through the skin can lead to the same issues. The toxin also causes skin irritation, as it's able to easily penetrate and damage the skin barrier. Sodium lauryl sulfate has been shown to contribute to contact dermatitis and to irritate skin conditions, like eczema and seborrhea.

Parabens

Potentially the most damaging of the toxic chemicals found in commercial soaps, parabens have been linked to birth defects, early puberty, hormonal cancers and organ toxicity. These toxins are not only found in soap; they work as preservatives in numerous cosmetic products, including makeup, deodorant and sunscreen. In fact, in a CDC report, a random sampling of 100 human urine specimens revealed parabens in all samples tested, which shows how heavily laden our products are with this dangerous toxin. Parabens have a high absorption rate and interfere with our body's hormonal balance. In breast cancer cells, parabens show estrogenic activity. The Journal of Applied Toxicology reported research which had determined that paraben esters were present in 99% of sampled breast cancer tissue, with five different paraben esters appearing in 60% of the sampled cases. Women, in particular, are susceptible to the destructive nature of parabens and should avoid them altogether.

Propylene Glycol

The fact that propylene glycol was initially used in anti-freeze should tell you something about how dangerous it can be in products for human use or consumption. And yet it is found in many processed foods and in many bodycare products. The use in the latter allows for an easy and inexpensive skin conditioning application of the product, due to propylene glycol's petroleum-based consistency. Propylene glycol does its duty in commercial soaps by preventing the product from drying out; but, in the process, it does significant damage to the liver and kidneys. The neurotoxin has also been shown to result in dermatitis. Further health issues caused by propylene glycol include gastrointestinal discomfort, headache, vomiting, nausea, skin and eye irritation, and central nervous system damage, according to the National Institute for Occupational Health and Safety.

DEA and TEA

DEA (diethanolamine) and TEA (triethanolamine) are incorporated in cosmetic products to balance the pH. When absorbed over time, DEA and TEA show toxicity, with the potential to damage the liver or kidneys and to produce allergic reactions. In Europe, the use of DEA and TEA in cosmetic products has even been banned due to their carcinogenic effects.

Phthalates

Used in everything from plastics to synthetic fragrances to medical goods, phthalates assist in the dissolution of ingredients, helping to form a balanced consistency in goods and products. However, the effectiveness of phthalates in this objective does not mean the chemical is safe. In fact, phthalates have been shown to contribute to birth defects, hormone imbalance and cell mutation.

Food, Drug and Cosmetic (FD&C) Colors

Although the artificial coloring in cosmetics is regulated and approved by the FDA, the derivatives they may contain have destructive potential. Coal tar derivatives, which are carcinogenic and allergy-inducing, are used in the production of some synthetic coloring. In natural products, you don't have to worry about synthetics at all.

Triclosan

Classified by the FDA as a pesticide, it comes as no surprise that triclosan produces health issues when used in bodycare products. Commonly used in store-bought soaps – as well as in gels and wipes – , the synthetic chemical's beneficial properties help kill bacteria; however, this antimicrobial toxin has been shown to interfere with thyroid function, produce hormone imbalance, cause dermatitis, irritate the skin, and has been classified by the Environmental Protection Agency as a potential carcinogen. Exposure to triclosan has even been shown to stimulate bacterial resistance to antibiotics, according to the American Medical Association.

Formaldehyde

This toxic chemical, along with its formaldehyde-releasing preservatives, is a common ingredient in a number of bodycare products. In cosmetics, formaldehyde serves to inhibit bacterial growth. However, formaldehyde has been classified by the International Agency for Research on Carcinogens (IARC) as a carcinogen, which is shown to cause nasal and nsopharyngeal cancers. Formaldehyde is also a skin allergin and may damage the immune system.

Fragrance

As a creative term to privatize a brand's "secret formula," the obscure "fragrance" ingredient listed on the packaging of many bodycare products could be shielding any number of toxins in the guise of scent. You, the consumer, have no idea what chemicals have been spliced together to compose this secret formula, and they could be potentially harmful. Various fragrance ingredients in consumer products have been shown to cause dermatitis, allergies, reproductive defects, and respiratory issues, according to the Environmental Working Group (EWG) Skin Deep Database.

Toluene

Used in paint thinner and to help dissolve paint, this toxic solvent should, logically, be nowhere near bodycare products. However, toluene is used in everything from soap to nail polish to hair color. Toluene is derived from coal tar or petroleum sources, and appears on products under the titles phenylmethane, benzene, methylbenzene, and toluol. The petrochemical is a known skin irritant and nausea-inducer. It has also been shown to damage the respiratory and immune systems. In pregnant mothers, toluene can cause mutations or fetus damage.

Chapter 2:
Things You Do Want to Put in Your Body: Potential Ingredients for Natural Soap

Antioxidants

Free radicals are destructive chemicals that invade your body, produced by substances both inside and out. Some free radicals (or oxidants) form from normal bodily reactions, like inflammation, metabolism and aerobic respiration. Other free radicals form from outside the body, but enter it due to exposure. These include harmful pollutants, toxins, smoking, drinking alcohol, X-rays, and UV rays, just to name a few. Although our bodies produce their own antioxidants, these often become damaged as we grow older; thus, introducing antioxidants into our bodies allow these nutrients and enzymes to assist in chemical reactions and destroy the oxidants or free radicals. So, basically, any product that's high in antioxidants has the potential to prevent or treat the development of chronic diseases that result from these free radicals – everything from arthritis to heart disease to cancer. This is why it is important to replace the toxins found in consumer products with natural ingredients, full of components that will aid our health, rather than destroy it.

Probiotics

Probiotics are "good bacteria" found in both food and supplements, and they positively influence digestion. Those who are health conscious know that a healthy body begins and ends with digestion. Fermented foods, such as kombucha and kefir, produce effective digestive systems, and the health craze has broken into the bodycare arena, as well, through the development of topical products.

Probiotics are increasingly being included in body products, as they aid the bacteria balance in your skin in much the same way that they aid the digestive balance of bacteria. People who have psoriasis, eczema, discoloration, acne, skin rashes or allergies can treat these skin issues with probiotics. Even further, those of us who are simply aging can do so gracefully, as probiotics help smooth out wrinkles.

As skin is the body's largest organ, doing all you can to protect it should go without saying. Disease-causing pathogens often make first contact with the skin, so priming your skin to put up guards against these harmful toxins should include promoting micro flora. Micro flora are positive bacteria which prevent the bad guys from breaking through the good guys' ranks.

Though consumer soap serves its purpose, it kills the "good guys" along with the bad, removing the barricades that our skin naturally provides. Being as such, creating a natural probiotic soap will not only help you avoid manslaughter, it will reinforce the good bacteria in your skin.

*If your natural soap recipe calls for probiotics, search for a supplement that is shelf stable and includes bifidobacteria and lactobacillus, good bacteria that is highly resistant.

Castile Soap

Castile soap can serve as a great base for your natural soap. Available for purchase in flake or liquid form, unlike other soaps which are made from animal fat, castile soap is generally a combination of hemp, jojoba, coconut and olive oil, while pure castile soap consists only of olive oil and may be the best for your base. Whether pure or blended, castile soap offers up a superb biodegradable, non-toxic, super green ingredient for your natural soap. Both soothing and gentle on the skin, castile soap also cleanses impurities from the skin, while retaining moisture and promoting elasticity.

Glycerin Soap

Glycerin soap is an all natural soap, free of synthetic ingredients. As one of the most moisturizing soaps that is compatible with all skin types, glycerin can serve as a great base for the melt-and-pour method. Glycerin soap is particularly soothing on sensitive skin.

Lye

Though on its own, lye is a caustic chemical that's harsh on skin, this ingredient is a common one in soaps, because when prepared and cured correctly, the chemical reaction lye has with a soap's oils helps create an effective cleanser. In the end, there is no lye in the completed product. Through the process of saponification (the combination of lye and the oils), glycerin is created along with the soap. In commercial products, glycerin is often removed from soap, manufactured, and sold to benefit other moisturizing products. But when you leave it in your natural homemade soap, you have a super moisturizing agent. However, it's important to note that if you're using lye in your soap making process, proceed with caution.

Distilled Water

Instead of using purified water or tap water in your soap recipe, use distilled to avoid the impurities and minerals the others contain. Mineral deposits from purified or tap water build up on the skin. These minerals are absent from distilled water, as they've been strained out through the distillation process.

Carrier Oils

Carrier oils will provide your soap a moisturizing base and also help dilute your essential oils. Almost all of the carrier oils mentioned have their own benefits, including anti-microbial and antifungal properties. This means they'll help rid your skin of environmental toxins, promote skin health, and can even help treat skin diseases, like eczema and psoriasis. The following carrier oils can be used effectively for skin health:

Coconut Oil - coconut oil is an extremely healthy oil when it comes to both dietary health and other health applications. With its high volume of antioxidants, coconut oil – like its essential oil counterparts – is effective in combating free radicals (see antioxidants).

Jojoba Oil – with vitamins A, D and E and antioxidants, jojoba oil promotes skin health by moisturizing and helping treat dry skin.

Olive Oil – olive oil probably has the longest history as a go-to oil for skin health. This multifaceted oil can restore glow, moisturize, fight fungus and bacteria, and boost blood flow.

Tamanu Oil – tamanu oil's antifungal and antioxidant properties mean it will help treat skin conditions while locking in moisture.

Sweet Almond Oil – high in vitamins E, B, D and A, almond oil provides an abundance of vitamins and nutrients to skin, providing your skin with a healthy glow.

Essential Oils

Last, but certainly not least, we arrive at essential oils. Essential oils are super concentrated aromatic liquids, so their scent is ultra potent. Not only will these natural oils enable you to customize the scent of your product, but they offer exceptional health benefits as well. These oils are deemed "essential", because the oils are composed of the "essence" of the plant. The difference between essential oils and other oils – like olive oil or vegetable oil, for instance – is that essential oils have high volatility and reduced fixation, which results in faster evaporation, enabling their popular use in aromatherapy. Even at high temperatures, olive and vegetable oils don't evaporate.

If you do a little research into your average century-old medical text, you will find that essential oils, herbs, and plenty of other natural ingredients have been used for thousands of years to treat any number of ailments and injuries. Though this sort of medicine is considered "alternative" now, it was once the gold standard. And perhaps it still should be, as these age-tested oils are safe, natural alternatives to the known or suspected carcinogens found in many consumer deodorants and other bodycare products.

Essential oils can be used as a supplement in soaps, as both a scent and as an additional health-boosting agent. When used topically, essential oils often require dilution with a carrier oil.

Chapter 3:
Pure Essential Oils & Blending Options

In this chapter, we'll discuss which essential oil blending options are particularly effective for specific skin conditions, as well as potential aromatic essential oil blending options. This list is, of course, not exhaustive. Within any of the recipes in the following chapters, you can incorporate or substitute one of our suggested scent blends or experiment with others that appeal to you. 30 drops of essential oil per 2 cups of liquid soap is sufficient. Here are a few recommendations to get you started.

Treatment Blending Options

Acne

Combine 20 drops lavender, 15 drops chamomile, and 15 drops calendula to help cleanse acne-prone skin.

Combine 20 drops lemon and 30 drops chamomile to soothe and cleanse acne and lighten skin spots.

Combine 25 drops orange and 25 drops rose to help treat acne-prone skin.

Combine 25 drops bergamot and 25 drops geranium for a great antiseptic soap that helps prevent acne.

Antibacterial

Combine 25 drops lemon and 25 drops cinnamon for a soap that's both antiviral and antibacterial.

Combine 20 drops basil, 15 drops rosemary, and 15 drops lemon for a great antibacterial soap.

Combine 25 drops tea tree with 25 drops lavender for an antiseptic soap that's also antiviral, antifungal and antibacterial.

Cellulite

Combine 20 drops lemon and 30 drops geranium to reduce water retention and cellulite.

Dry Skin

Combine 25 drops rose and 25 drops chamomile to soothe dry skin.

Combine 20 drops jasmine, 15 drops patchouli, and 15 drops lavender to create a soothing soap for dry skin.

Dull Skin

Combine 25 drops orange with 25 drops patchouli to nourish and rejuvenate dull skin.

Irritated Skin

Combine 25 drops tea tree with 25 drops geranium for an antibacterial soap that helps treat irritated skin.

Combine 25 drops orange with 25 drops basil to help treat irritated skin.

Skin Conditions

Combine 25 drops basil and 25 drops lavender to create an antiseptic and antibacterial soap that helps treat psoriasis and eczema.

Combine 20 drops geranium, 15 drops orange, and 15 drops patchouli to help treat skin condition like eczema, psoriasis, or dermatitis. Also soothes dry skin.

Stress

Combine 25 drops ylang-ylang with 25 drops bergamot to create a great de-stressing soap.

Combine 25 drops lemon with 25 drops lavender to help unwind.

Combine 15 drops orange, 25 drops peppermint, and 10 drops eucalyptus for a minty fresh stress reducer.

Combine 30 drops lavender, 15 drops orange, and 5 drops clove (or cinnamon) to calm stress.

Wrinkles or Scars

Combine 20 drops sandalwood, 15 drops orange, and 15 drops geranium to help improve skin issues, like scars, wrinkles or stretch marks.

Aromatic Blend Options

If your skin is naturally healthy, you may be using essential oils in your soap recipe primarily for the scent. Here are some aromatic combinations that blend well together to form a complementary aroma.

Classic Blends

For a classic scent, combine 15 drops geranium, 15 drops cedarwood, 10 drops patchouli, and 10 drops tea tree essential oils.

A second classic scent combines 25 drops frankincense with 25 drops of ylang-ylang.

A third option combines 10 drops lemon, 15 drops lavender and 25 drops lemongrass.

A fourth option combines 30 drops wild orange with 20 drops lavender.

A fifth option combines 30 drops lavender with 20 drops peppermint.

Flowery Blends

For a fresh, flowery blend, combine 10 drops rosemary, 10 drops lemon and 30 drops lavender.

A second flowery scent combines 20 drops vanilla with 30 drops lavender.

Another option combines 25 drops geranium with 25 drops sweet orange.

Musky Blend

For a deep, musky scent, combine 20 drops sandalwood with 30 drops frankincense.

Combine 25 drops sandalwood with 25 drops patchouli for a strong, rich scent.

Sultry Blends

A sultry feminine blend combines 25 drops rose with 25 drops geranium.

A second sultry scent combines 25 drops jasmine with 25 drops ylang ylang.

You can also combine 15 drops chamomile, 15 drops lemongrass and 20 drops lemon.

Combine 20 drops frankincense, 15 drops myrrh and 15 drops rose.

Combine 20 drops chamomile, 15 drops patchouli, and 15 drops ylang-ylang.

Combine 20 drops rose, 15 drops patchouli and 15 drops jasmine.

Citrus Blends

A fresh citrus blend combines 25 drops sweet orange with 25 drops lemon.

A second option combines 30 drops tea tree, 10 drops lemon, and 10 drops lemongrass.

A third option combines 15 drops orange, 10 drops grapefruit, 15 drops mandarin and 10 drops lemon.

Soothing Blends

A soothing blend combines 15 drops geranium, 25 drops lavender, and 10 drops Roman Chamomile.

A second option combines 15 drops lavender, 25 drops bergamot, and 10 drops marjoram.

A third option combines 20 drops sandalwood, 15 drops jasmine, and 15 drops geranium.

A fourth option combines 25 drops chamomile and 25 drops lavender. Gentle enough for sensitive skin.

Invigorating Blend

This invigorating blend combines 15 drops pine, 25 drops lemon, and 10 drops frankincense.

Combine 20 drops jasmine, 15 drops frankincense and 15 drops geranium for an invigorating and uplifting blend.

Combine 25 drops mint with 25 drops basil to re-energize and invigorate.

Combine 25 drops tea tree with 25 drops orange.

We Recommend...

Whichever blend of essential oils you choose, consider throwing one of the following oils into the mix, as they are high in antibacterial and antiseptic properties:

- lemon

- lemongrass

- lavender

- thyme

- rosemary

- tea tree

- geranium

For masculine scents or blends, we recommend incorporating any of the following essential oils:

- peppermint

- frankincense

- cinnamon

- cedarwood

- marjoram

- bay

- cardamon

- pine

- myrrh

- ginger

- juniper

When you experiment with different blends, do not go overboard. Start with a few drops of your selected oils and then smell-test. You can always add a few more drops, but if you overdo it, you'll have wasted a lot of oil, and you'll probably have created too strong a scent, which means you'll have to start from scratch. It's also important to consider the strength of each oil in order to determine the amount of drops. For instance, the scents of lemongrass and lemon are strong, which means if you add equal parts of lemon to any other essential oil of lesser strength, it will overpower the lighter scent. On the other hand, lavender is subdued and would take more drops than some other oils to make its mark. Consider oil strength when experimenting with portion sizes in your blends.

Chapter 4:
Herbs

The recipes in this book may call for flowers and herbs. The addition of herbs to your soap can both complement the scent of your essential oils and provide their own effective properties to reinforce the health of your skin. You can buy herbs either fresh or dry; there is no difference in their properties.

Chamomile

Chamomile is actually related to the native Eastern European sunflower, found primarily in Croatia, Hungary, and Serbia. Egyptian chamomile was used medicinally by the native peoples, as well as by the Romans and the Greeks. Modern applications, include those in tea, health products, and cosmetics, with nearly one million pounds being used in tea in the US each year. The most common chamomile used is German chamomile, while Roman chamomile is more expensive due to its relative rarity.

Rosemary

This culinary spice is in the mint family and is native to the Mediterranean. Rosemary's evergreen needle leaves are used in medicine and food and are easily cultivated, thriving in sunny environments with dry soil. No matter the chemotype, rosemary's scent and flavor is similar across the board.

Calendula

Native to the Mediterranean regions in the north, calendula blooms each month with the new moon. Ancient Egyptians believed calendula flowers to be rejuvenating, while the Hindus believed them to be spiritually uplifting, influencing them to decorate their temples and statues with the flower. Also referred to as a "marigold," the name is derived by its Catholic roots in its connection with the Virgin Mary. Calendula is presently used in cosmetics, fabrics and food as a coloring agent and, in the 18th century, was even applied as such to cheese.

Lavender

Also native to the Mediterranean, this evergreen shrub is presently cultivated in the US and Europe, blooming its purple flowers from the latter end of spring to the early part of autumn. The ancient Egyptians used lavender in mummification thousands of years ago, while the ancient Greeks and Romans applied it to cosmetics, perfumes, insect repellants, baking and cooking, and for medicinal purposes. The name "lavender" is derived from the Latin word for "to wash," which is "lavare," because the Romans used it as an after-wash. Grave robbers used a mixture containing lavender, called Four Thieves, so that they would not become infected during the Great Plague in 1665. The mixture also contained vinegar, wormwood, sage, rue, rosemary and mint.

Comfrey

Comfrey's leaves have been used for over 2,000 years in traditional Chinese medicine. During the Middle Ages, comfrey baths were all the fad, and this herb became known as "one of nature's greatest medicinal herbs."

Lemon & Orange Peel

The cut and dried outer skin of the lemon or orange has long been used in Ayurvedic and Chinese medicine in digestion. When ingested or applied topically, both provide the body vitamin C.

Nettle Leaf

This botanical, native to western Asia and Africa, consists of stinging hairs which defend against predators.

The hairs produce somewhat painful stinging welts if touched, which swell due to the nettle's formic acid. The welts don't last long or cause too much pain, as the acid and potency of the stinging hairs quickly diminishes. The leaves harvested from the picking are worth any pain. They've been used medicinally and in the production of foods and fabrics for ages.

Oregano

This warm, bitter herb of the mint family is best grown in warm climates with lots of sunlight, which is perhaps why the Greek derivation of the name means "mountain of joy." The pungency of oregano numbs the tongue.

Plantain

The plantain is amongst the Saxon's nine sacred herbs, and is considered an aphrodisiac today. Though many cultures promote the benefits of plantain, in some areas where plantain is not native, it's referred to as a noxious weed.

Rose Petals and/or Leaves

Being that the rose is most powerful on the first morning that the flower opens, rose petals are picked at that time; afterwards, the flower quickly deteriorates due to the wind and sun. Rose petals will provide your soap with a perfume-like scent and a lovely color.

Sage

Popular in cooking, sage is used as a flavoring agent in almost all European cuisine, but it's also known for its medicinal properties. "Salvia," its Latin name is derived from the word "to heal."

Thyme

Originating in the southern Mediterranean, thyme is an aromatic herb that now thrives throughout North America as well. The Greek derivation of thyme was "thumus," or "courage." During the middle ages, knights attached thyme to their armor to symbolize their courage, and the scent is said to have provided strength in battle.

Violet Flowers and/or Leaves

Used for centuries in traditional folk medicine, violets were applied to "love potion" by the Greeks, as the perfume was thought to influence love and fertility. The flowers and leaves can also be used in culinary dishes and herbal medicines.

Chapter 5:
Getting Started

Gather Your Materials

For the recipes in this book, you will generally need the below materials:

- Scale (to measure out your ingredients)
- Measuring Cups
- Pyrex Jug
- Steel Pan
- 2 Wooden Spoons
- Stick Blender
- Candy Thermometer
- Rubber Gloves
- Safety Goggles
- Silicone Molds

- Greaseproof Paper
- Mason Jar
- Soap Dispenser

Choose a Soap Base

If you're using the melt-and-pour method for your all-natural product, select a soap base that contains natural vegetable components, like glycerin soap. Glycerin soap is composed of olive and coconut oils, among other things. Goat's milk glycerin soap is particularly handy if you want to add herbs or botanicals, as instead of sinking to the bottom, the particles will be suspended.

Liquid castile soap also serves as a great soap base for liquid soap. Though it's thin in consistency, you can add a couple tablespoons of vegetable glycerin to thicken the base. Using soap flakes or grated olive oil soap bar can also serve as a consistent soap base. Whenever you'd like to adjust the consistency of homemade liquid soaps, you should experiment with the amount of water in the recipe. Of course, if you want a thinner liquid soap to use for dish soap or detergent, use more water; if you want thicker hand soap or bodywash, use less.

Choose a Mold

You can either buy silicone molds that are specifically manufactured for soap making or use muffin tins, ramekins, or other pans already on hand. If you use a loaf pan, you'll have to cut up the soap bars by hand, whereas if you use the other molds mentioned, you'll create ready-made single-sized soaps. Spray the molds with olive oil before filling them with the soap mixture to enable easy removal of the soap bars.

Safety Instructions & Helpful Tips

- Bar soap is often made by mixing lye and water with an oil mixture. The two mixtures do not blend easily and require attention to the temperatures (usually 110 ° F for both the lye mixture and the oil mixture). Heat the oil gently and pay attention to the temperature of your lye as it cools.
- With recipes that use lye, proceed with caution, as it will react with the water and, as the reaction occurs, can be caustic to skin. Combine chemicals in a well ventilated area, isolated from children and pets.
- Always wear safety goggles and gloves when the ingredients you work with involve chemical reactions.
- Clean all materials thoroughly. If practical, keep soap-making materials separate from those with which you cook food. If you plan on making soap frequently, having designated materials for the process will eliminate cross-contamination.
- Always measure ingredients carefully, as the recipes often require precise accuracy.
- Soap is done when your mixture reaches "trace." This is a state where a small film of the soap

remains on the surface of the mixture, sort of like pudding. Being aware of this state will inform you when your soap is ready to pour into the molds.

- If you want to determine how much soap will fill a specific mold, then simply fill the mold with water and pour the water into a measuring cup.

- Do not overcook or burn your soap. Doing so will result in a bad odor and discoloration.

- Do not over-stir your soap. Doing so will increase bubbles. Instead, stir slowly in a circular motion.

- Never microwave molds, and ensure that your soap is not too hot before pouring. This will prevent warping.

- Do not use molds composed of colored or weak plastic, tin, aluminum, zinc, untempered glass or china. Weak plastic might melt, colored plastic might result in your soaps discoloration, metals might corrode, and china and untempered glass might shatter.

- If you've prepared your molds properly, soap should be easily removed. If it isn't, place in the freezer for ten minutes to cool and solidify and remove without onto the drying surface without touching the soaps, otherwise your fingerprints will be visible on the soap's wet surface.

- Do not use food dye or coloring unless specific to soap making. Food grade coloring will stain washing materials and your skin.

- If you're adding essential oils to a heated soap, add only after the soap has cooled to below 120° F, as the scent will burn off otherwise. Preferably add the EOs right before pouring the soap into molds.

- When melting soap, always use enameled pans, stainless steel, or microwave-safe glass. Never use aluminum.

- Do not touch soap bare-handed until the mixture has cooled.

- If you've created too much soap for your molds, do not scrap the excess. Pour into any available container and store for a future project. You can always remelt and reuse.

- Botanicals or herbs should be added only once the soap has cooled and thickened a bit. Do not add too much, as the soap will become abrasive, and keep the particles suspended by stirring constantly. If you're using flower petals, such as rose or lavender, make sure the botanicals haven't browned or rotted after a few days.

- If you're adding herbs or essential oils, the color of the additives may influence the final color of your soap. Keep this in mind if you're looking to produce a certain tinge.

- To reduce surface bubbles, spray the soaps lightly with rubbing alcohol after pouring them in their molds. Alternatively, you can lightly brush the tops of the soap with a spoon to eliminate bubbles.

- Clean and dry molds after use, and store silicone molds in a cool, dark cupboard.

Chapter 6:
Natural Bar Soap Recipes

Calendula in the Lemongrass Soap

Makes 4 bars

Ingredients

- 16 ounces Clear Glycerin Soap
- 2 Tbsp Dried Calendula Petals
- 3 drops Yellow Soap Coloring
- 10-15 drops Lemongrass Essential Oil

Directions

Spray your muffin cups, ramekins or other chosen

molds with olive oil and set aside. Place the glycerin soap in a glass bowl or mason jar and place bowl into a saucepan with 1 inch of water over low to medium heat. Stir soap regularly until melted. Remove from heat and add in soap coloring and essential oils, stirring until evenly blended. Let cool somewhat before stirring in your calendula petals, ensuring that they are entirely encased in the soap. Pour the mixture into the molds and allow to set until hardened, or around 25 minutes. Press the soaps out with your thumb or a knife and store them in a ziplock bag or plastic wrap.

Chamomile Oatmeal Soap

Makes 4 bars

Ingredients

- 16 ounces Clear Glycerin Soap
- 2 Tbsp Oats
- 2 Tbsp Dried Lavender Petals
- 2 drops Red Soap Coloring
- 1 drop Blue Soap Coloring
- 5 drops Roman Chamomile Essential Oil
- 10 drops Lavender Essential Oil

Directions

Spray your muffin cups, ramekins or other chosen molds with olive oil and set aside. Place the glycerin soap in a glass bowl or mason jar and place bowl into a saucepan with 1 inch of water over low to medium heat. Stir soap regularly until melted. Remove from heat and add in soap coloring and essential oils, stirring until evenly blended. Let cool somewhat before stirring in your lavender petals, ensuring that they are entirely encased in the soap. Pour the mixture into the molds and allow to set until hardened, or around 25 minutes. Press the soaps out with your thumb or a knife and store them in a ziplock bag or plastic wrap.

Coconut Tea Tree Soap

Ingredients

- 16 ounces Distilled Water
- 10 ounces Coconut Oil
- 40 ounces Grapeseed Oil Blend
- 6.9 ounces Lye
- 1 ounce Tea Tree Essential Oil
- Directions

Spray your muffin cups, ramekins or other chosen molds with olive oil and set aside. Place the lye and water into a disposable container and set aside. Place the coconut and grapeseed oils in a glass bowl or mason jar and place container into a saucepan with 1 inch of water over low to medium heat. Stir oils regularly until melted and well combined. Remove from heat and add in lye-water mixture, stirring until the combination is cloudy. When the mixture is cloudy, begin to pulse blend the mixture with an immersion blender. After a few minutes, blend evenly until the mixture starts to thicken. Add in the essential oil and blend until it has further thickened. When the mixture is well combined, pour it into the molds and allow to set for 3-4 days. When the soap is solid, press the soaps out with your thumb or a knife and let sit for 7-10 days or until hardened. Store them in a ziplock bag or plastic wrap.

Flower Garden Soap

Makes 8-12 bars

Ingredients

- 20 ounces Olive Oil
- 7.5 ounces Distilled Water
- 2.5 ounces Lye
- 15 drops Rose Essential Oil
- 15 drops Geranium Essential Oil

Directions

In a jug, combine water and lye, stirring until well combined (caution: combination will heat). Set aside. In a pan, heat olive oil over medium heat, until it reaches 110 ° F. Check using a candy thermometer. Check the lye-water mixture with the thermometer. When it has reached 110 ° F as well, add it slowly to the oil. Blend together until well combined. Stir in essential oils. When the mixture reaches a thickened consistency, "trace" will appear – a faint layer that settles atop the mixture. This means it's ready. Pour the mixture into the molds and allow to set until hardened, covering with greaseproof paper and topping the paper with a tea towel for two days. Once hardened, press the soaps out with your thumb or a knife and allow them to "cure" for five weeks before use. Once cured, store them in a ziplock bag or plastic wrap.

Rich Rose-Scented Soap

Ingredients

- 700 mL Distilled Water
- 9 ¼ ounces Lye
- 2 cups Grapeseed Oil
- 2 cups Coconut Oil
- 4 ½ cups Olive Oil
- 2 Tbsp Dried Rose Petals
- 10 drops Frankincense Essential Oil
- 10 drops Myrrh Essential Oil
- 10 drops Rose Essential Oil

Directions

In a jug, combine water and lye, stirring until well combined (caution: combination will heat). Set aside. In a pan, heat olive oil over low medium heat, until it reaches 110 ° F. Check using a candy thermometer. Check the lye-water mixture with the thermometer. When it has reached 110 ° F as well, add it slowly to the oil. Blend together until well combined. Stir in essential oils and dried rose petals. When the mixture reaches a thickened consistency, "trace" will appear – a faint layer that settles atop the mixture. This means it's ready. Pour the mixture into the molds and allow to set until hardened, covering with greaseproof paper and wrapping the paper with a towel for 24 hours. Once hardened, press the soaps out with your thumb or a knife and allow them to "cure" for five weeks before use. Turn them over after two weeks.

Soft & Soothing Soap

Ingredients

- 5 ounces Lye
- 7 ounces Palm Oil
- 10 ½ ounces Coconut Oil
- 17 ounces Olive Oil
- 13 ounces Distilled Water
- 2 Tbsp Dried Lavender Petals
- 20 drops Chamomile Essential Oil
- 20 drops Lavender Essential Oil

Directions

Line your muffin cups, ramekins or other chosen molds with freezer paper (shiny side facing the soaps) and set aside. In a jug, combine water and lye, stirring until well combined (caution: combination will heat). Set aside. In a pan, heat palm, coconut and olive oil over low medium heat, stirring often until well blended. Once it reaches 110 ° F (check using a candy thermometer), remove from stove. Check the lye-water mixture with the thermometer. When it has reached 110 ° F as well, add it slowly to the oil. Blend together until well combined. Stir in essential oils and dried lavender petals. When the mixture reaches a thickened consistency, "trace" will appear – a faint layer that settles atop the mixture. This means it's ready. Pour the mixture into the molds and allow to set until hardened, covering with greaseproof paper and wrapping the paper with a towel for 24 hours. Once hardened, press the soaps out with your thumb or a knife and allow them to "cure" for five weeks before use. Turn them over after two weeks.

Invigorating Soap

Ingredients

- ¼ cup Lye
- 2/3 cup Almond Oil
- 2/3 cup Coconut Oil
- 2/3 cup Olive Oil
- ¾ cup Distilled Water
- 20 drops Mint Essential Oil
- 20 drops Basil Essential Oil

Directions

Line your muffin cups, ramekins or other chosen molds with freezer paper (shiny side facing the soaps) and set aside. In a jug, combine water and lye, stirring until well combined (caution: combination will heat). Set aside. In a large mason jar, pour almond, coconut and olive oil. Place jar in 1 inch of water in a saucepan and heat over low medium heat, stirring often until well blended. Once it reaches 110 ° F (check using a candy thermometer), remove from stove. Check the lye-water mixture with the thermometer. When it has reached 110 ° F as well, add it slowly to the oil. Blend together until well combined. Stir in essential oils. When the mixture reaches a thickened consistency, "trace" will appear – a faint layer that settles atop the mixture. This means it's ready. Pour the mixture into the molds and allow to set until hardened, covering with greaseproof paper and wrapping the paper with a towel for 24 hours. Once hardened, press the soaps out with your thumb or a knife and allow them to "cure" for five weeks before use. Turn them over after two weeks. Once cured, store wrapped in wax paper or in an airtight container

Chapter 7:
Natural Liquid Hand soap Recipes

Citrus Blend Hand soap

Ingredients

- 2 Tbsp Liquid Castile Soap
- 1 Tbsp Fractionated Coconut Oil
- 3 drops Orange Essential Oil
- 2 drops Grapefruit Essential Oil
- 3 drops Mandarin Essential Oil
- 2 drops Lemon Essential Oil
- Distilled Water

Directions

In an empty glass soap dispenser or pump bottle, pour the coconut oil with the castile soap. Cap and shake well to combine. Next, add in the essential oils and fill the bottle ¾ full with water so that the pump may be placed without overflowing the soap. Place the pump securely and shake well.

Invigorating Antibacterial Hand soap

Makes 4-6 bars and 1 litre liquid soap

Ingredients

Part I

- 10 ounces Olive Oil
- 3.75 ounces Distilled Water
- 1.25 ounces Lye
- 7 drops Cinnamon Essential Oil
- 7 drops Lemon Essential Oil

Part II

- 20 mL Glycerin
- 1 L Distilled Water
- 7 drops Cinnamon Essential Oil
- 7 drops Lemon Essential Oil

Directions

In a jug, combine water and lye, stirring until well combined (caution: combination will heat). Set aside. In a pan, heat olive oil over low medium heat, until it reaches 110 ° F. Check using a candy thermometer. Check the lye-water mixture with the thermometer. When it has reached 110 ° F as well, add it slowly to the oil. Blend together until well combined. Stir in essential oils. When the mixture reaches a thickened consistency, "trace" will appear – a faint layer that settles atop the mixture. This means it's ready. Pour the mixture into the molds and allow to set until hardened, covering with greaseproof paper and wrapping the paper with a towel for two days. Once hardened, press the soaps out with your thumb or a knife and allow them to "cure" for five weeks before use. Once cured, you can now use one of the bars to make liquid soap and store the rest in a ziplock bag or plastic wrap for future use.

Grate one of the olive oil bars with a food processor. Place 1 litre of water into a pan and bring to a boil. Pour half of the water into a glass bowl. Return the pan to the stove and, on low medium heat, stir in the grated soap flakes. Combine until melted and remove from heat. Add in the remaining water, blending to remove lumps. Let cool and then stir again with the blender. Mix in the glycerin and essential oils. Allow to cool completely before pouring some of the soap into an empty glass soap dispenser or pump bottle. Fill the bottle ¾ full so that the pump may be placed without overflowing the soap. Place the pump securely and shake well.

Minty Fresh Hand soap

Ingredients

- 1 cup Glycerin Soap
- ½ Tbsp Vegetable Glycerin
- ½ tsp Vitamin E
- 15 drops Peppermint Essential Oil
- 10 drops Orange Essential Oil
- 5 drops Eucalyptus Essential Oil
- 1 drop Ylang Ylang Essential Oil
- 5 cups Distilled Water

Directions

Finely grate the glycerin bar into a large pot. Over low medium heat, add in the water and vegetable glycerin. Stir until melted and well blended. Allow to cool for 12 hours. The consistency should be lumpy. With an electric hand mixer, blend the soap until smooth, stirring in the essential oils and vitamin E until well combined. In an empty glass soap dispenser or pump bottle, pour the soap until ¾ full so that the pump may be placed without overflowing the soap. Place the pump securely and shake well. Use as needed, and store remainder in a cool dark cupboard.

Face-Cleansing Soap

Ingredients

- ½ cup Castile Soap
- 5 tsp Jojoba or Sunflower Oil
- 1 cup Distilled Water
- 2 Tbsp Organic Honey
- 1 Tbsp Tea Tree Essential Oil
- 15 drops Lemon Essential Oil
- *adjust ingredients per your skin type (ie, more castile/less water if you have oily skin, avoid

Directions

Add the castile soap to the water. Stir, then add the oil and honey. Combine the rest, stirring gently. In an empty glass soap dispenser or pump bottle, pour the soap until ¾ full so that the pump may be placed without overflowing the soap. Place the pump securely and shake well. Use as needed, and store remainder in a cool dark cupboard.

Musky Soap

Ingredients

- 5.5 ounces Potassium Hydroxide
- 7 ounces Coconut Oil
- 16.5 ounces Olive Oil
- 3 ounces Borax
- 62.5 ounces Distilled Water (divided)
- 20 drops Patchouli Essential Oil
- 20 drops Sandalwood Essential Oil

Directions

Line your muffin cups, ramekins or other chosen molds with freezer paper (shiny side facing the soaps) and set aside. In a slow cooker, place coconut and olive oil, stirring until well combined. Heat on low. Pour water into a separate jug and slowly stir in potassium hydroxide until dissolved. When clear, add potassium hydroxide mixture to the slow cooker. Blend together for about 5 minutes until well combined. When the mixture reaches a thickened consistency, "trace" will appear – a faint layer that settles atop the mixture. This means it's ready. Place lid on the slow cooker and allow to cook for 30 minutes. Check if the mixture has separated. If it has, stir again and allow to set again. Cook for 3-4 hours, checking and stirring every 30 minutes. The consistency will alter every thirty minutes, transitioning from an apple sauce to a custard-like consistency, then from mashed potatoes to taffy, and from creamy petroleum jelly to translucent petroleum jelly. Once you've reached the final stage, test it by adding 1 ounce of the soap to 2 ounces water. Mix until dissolved and allow to set for a couple minutes. If the water is clear-to-slightly cloudy, then it's ready. If very cloudy, allow to cook for another 30 minutes or more and test again. Once it's clear, bring 40 ounces of distilled water to a boil in a large pot. Pour in the mixture and stir or mash with a potato masher. When well combined, turn off heat and place the lid on the pot. Let sit for an hour, then stir. If it's still chunky, let sit for an hour more and check again. When it's reached a smooth consistency, in a separate pot, bring 2 ounces of distilled water to a boil and dissolve 1 ounce of borax in it. Add ½ ounce of the borax mixture at a time to the soap base, stirring until you've added 2 ounces. Stir in essential oils. Pour soap into a gallon size mason jar. Secure and allow to sit for a week, so that the sediment may sink to the bottom. Once the soap clears, pour into an empty glass soap dispenser or pump bottle, until ¾ full so that the pump may be placed without overflowing the soap. Place the pump securely and shake well. Use as needed, and store remainder in a cool dark cupboard. Can be used for body wash or hand soap.

Chapter 8:
Natural Liquid Hand soap Recipes

Citrus Dish Soap

Ingredients

- ½ cup Castile Soap
- ½ Tbsp Vegetable Glycerin
- 4 cups Water
- 20 drops Tea Tree Essential Oil
- 10 drops Lemon Essential Oil
- 10 drops Lemongrass Essential Oil

Directions

Grate the glycerin soap. In a saucepan, pour distilled
water and grated soap and combine over low to
medium heat until melted. Stir in vegetable glycerin.
When blended, remove from heat and pour the
mixture into a glass container or mason jar. Let cool
for up to one hour. Add in essential oils, stirring until
evenly blended. Allow to set for up to 24 hours before
use, stirring occasionally. Shake before use.

Lavender Dish Soap

Great for cutting grease

Ingredients

- ¼ cup Castile Soap
- ¼ cup Soap Flakes
- 2 tsp Super Washing Soda
- 2 cups Distilled Water
- 1 tsp Vegetable Glycerin
- 30-40 drops Lavender Essential Oil

Directions

In a large saucepan, bring the water to a boil and stir in the soap flakes until dissolved. Add in remaining ingredients, stirring until dissolved and well combined. In an empty glass soap dispenser or pump bottle, pour the soap until ¾ full so that the pump may be placed without overflowing the soap. Place the pump securely and shake well. Let sit for 24 hours before use. Use as needed, shaking before each use, and store remainder in a cool dark cupboard.

Vinegar Dish Soap

Great for cutting grease

Ingredients

- ½ cup White Vinegar
- ½ cup Dr. Bronner's Sal Suds
- ½ cup Distilled Water
- 2 tsp Kosher Salt
- 1 tsp Citric Acid (may substitute Lemon Juice)
- 15 drops Orange Essential Oil
- 15 drops Lemon Essential Oil

Directions

In a medium bowl, warm the water in the microwave. Add salt and stir until dissolved. In a separate bowl, stir together vinegar, Sal Suds, and citric acid until well combined. Pour mixture into the salt water and mix until the combination thickens. Once it's thickened, add the essential oils and stir again. In an empty glass soap dispenser or pump bottle, pour the soap until ¾ full so that the pump may be placed without overflowing the soap. Place the pump securely and shake well. Let sit for 24 hours before use. Use as needed, shaking before each use, and store remainder in a cool dark cupboard.

Borax Dish Soap

Great for cutting grease

Ingredients

- 1 Tbsp Grated Soap
- 1 Tbsp Borax
- 1 ¾ cup Distilled Water
- 10 drops Orange Essential Oil
- 5 drops Grapefruit Essential Oil
- 10 drops Mandarin Essential Oil
- 5 drops Lemon Essential Oil

Directions

In a saucepan, bring the water to a boil. In a medium bowl, stir together grated bar soap and borax until well combined. Pour water into the mix and whisk until soap is melted and blended. Once it's thickened, add the essential oils and stir again. Let sit for 6-8 hours, stirring occasionally. In an empty glass soap dispenser or pump bottle, pour the soap until ¾ full so that the pump may be placed without overflowing the soap. Place the pump securely and shake well. Use as needed, shaking before each use, and store remainder in a cool dark cupboard.

Flowery Dish Soap

Great for cutting grease

Ingredients

- 1 Tbsp Borax
- 2 Tbsp White Vinegar
- 1 Tbsp Washing Soda
- ½ cup Liquid Castile Soap
- 2 ½ cups Distilled Water
- 10 drops Geranium Essential Oil
- 10 drops Rose Essential Oil

Directions

In a medium bowl, combine washing soda, borax, liquid castile soap and white vinegar. Mix well. Boil the water and slowly whisk in mixture. Turn down the heat and stir thoroughly until well combined. Once it's thickened, add the essential oils and stir again. Remove from heat and allow to sit for 6-8 hours. In an empty glass soap dispenser or pump bottle, pour the soap until ¾ full so that the pump may be placed without overflowing the soap. Place the pump securely and shake well. Let sit for 24 hours before use. Use as needed, shaking before each use, and store remainder in a cool dark cupboard.

CONCLUSION

As this book of recipes demonstrates, many natural alternatives to store-bought soaps exist. Some are easy, requiring no more than a few ingredients. Some are more complex, involving oils and scents that you're not likely to find in your pantry or medicine cabinet. However, it's important to note that, whichever recipe you choose, you can rest assured that you're creating a product with all natural ingredients which are not harmful or harsh, like those you'll find in commercial soaps.

There are a few things to note when making and using natural soaps:

Though the ingredients are natural, it must be mentioned that if you have sensitive skin or allergies, always err on the side of caution by consulting with a physician before using herbs or oils and seek help if you experience a reaction. Always test a small amount of the homemade product on your inner arm before applying regularly.

Unlike commercial products which are laden with chemicals to preserve the product's shelf-life, natural products live for a shorter time, so it's smart to make smaller portion sizes of your soap and do your best to extend its shelf life, by storing it properly (in an airtight glass container). We suggest that you store your batches of liquid soap in a mason jar in a cool, dry place and fill a reusable soap bottle with enough to last you a week or two.

Most natural soap recipes are good for at least 6 months if stored properly.

It should also be mentioned that natural soaps do not contain lathering or thickening agents like store-bought soaps, so they are not likely to be the same consistency or to lather the same way as commercial products. Many commercial soaps contain sodium lauryl sulfate, a lathering agent which produces the suds. Bubbles are not necessary for cleanliness, however, so there's no need to worry if your natural soap does not seem so sudsy.

Now that you know all about natural ingredients – how they will not only stimulate your skin, but will benefit your overall health, as well – you can get started experimenting with the soap recipes in this book or tweak them in order to invent your own. One of the many benefits of producing your own natural bodycare products is that you can customize your scent, as well as adjust the strength of scent. We recommend that you purchase your scents from doTERRA, which offers superior quality, therapeutic-grade essential oils.

The benefits of essential oils and their properties are countless. Used as a supplement, the applications of essential oils in bodycare products and medicine have survived for centuries and will survive many more. When it comes down to it, you don't need to rely on consumer products; essential oils, herbs, and plenty of other natural ingredients can be substituted for the toxic chemicals and carcinogens you'll find in store-bought brands.

DISCLAIMER AND/OR LEGAL NOTICES: Every effort has been made to accurately represent this book and it's potential. Results vary with every individual, and your results may or may not be different from those depicted. No promises, guarantees or warranties, whether stated or implied, have been made that you will produce any specific result from this book. Your efforts are individual and unique, and may vary from those shown. Your success depends on your efforts, background and motivation.

The material in this publication is provided for educational and informational purposes only and is not intended as medical advice. The information contained in this book should not be used to diagnose or treat any illness, metabolic disorder, disease or health problem. Always consult your physician or health care provider before beginning any nutrition or exercise program. Use of the programs, advice, and information contained in this book is at the sole choice and risk of the reader.